MUD ON MY BOOTS

The Estuaries and Countryside of the Norfolk Heritage Coast

by

Hugh Brandon-Cox

This book is dedicated to Janet whose wide knowledge of north Norfolk helped me to find suitable painting scenes.

BOOKS BY THE AUTHOR

Wanderings with the Woodman	Thames Publishing, London
Trail of the Arctic Nomads	Wm. Kimber, London
Summer of a Million Wings	David and Charles, Devon
Hovran (Swedish Bird Lake)	Tidens, Stockholm
Lure of the Wilderness	East Countryman

Published by
East Countryman
Bessingham, Norfolk, NR11 7JR, England
Telephone: +44 (0)1263 577777

ISBN 0-9543136-0-7

Designed and printed in England by
Barnwell's Print Ltd, Barnwell's Printing Works
Penfold Street, Aylsham, Norfolk, NR11 6ET
Telephone: +44 (0)1263 732767

Cover: *'Geese Coming in at Dusk to the Saltings'*
Frontispiece: *'The Lone Fisher'*

HUGH BRANDON-Cox

Foreword

HUGH BRANDON-COX has been a regular visitor to NWT Cley Marshes over the years and I have enjoyed many informative and interesting conversations with him on the boardwalk about our wonderful bird life. I am delighted to have been asked to write this foreword as Hugh's paintings and writing illustrate so clearly the luminous mists of the north Norfolk coast and its grey estuaries. I have never minded the mud and nor, I think, has Hugh!

I have spent my life on the north Norfolk coast and, like Hugh, it will always be close to my heart. My grandfather Robert, father Billy and myself have nurtured and developed NWT Cley Marshes for its bird life for over 70 years. The nature reserve is indeed a truly magical place. It is frequently described as a 'mecca' for birdwatchers, and deservedly so. Keeping the habitat in prime condition for our resident and visiting breeding birds is a skilled task. Norfolk Wildlife Trust strives to protect and enhance Norfolk's wildlife and wild places for people, and so the appreciation of regular visitors such as Hugh Brandon-Cox makes our task worthwhile.

Bernard Bishop
Warden
NWT Cley Marshes

'Waxwings on the coast in Winter from Scandinavia'

HUGH BRANDON-COX

Chapter One

Ebb-Tide and the Distant Past

WITH a grim relentless fury the wind stung my face, bringing a smarting to the eyes. Howling direct from the cold steppes of Siberia it reached this open mudscape at Brancaster with a low moaning anger.

Ebb-tide brings to this great exposed expanse of shifting sands, saltings, sucking mud-flats and gurgling creeks on the north Norfolk coast a huge vista empty of all humans on this bleak day.

Snow had begun to fall and the sky was grim with a deep darkest blue-grey before the oncome of the night. I began to retrace the deep mud-gripped footprints left earlier as I had plodded out as far as possible towards the far distant horizon.

Sullen winter had returned once more to this coastal region, bringing with it multitudes of wild wings gathered from their breeding sites as distant as Greenland, Siberia, Scandinavia, Iceland and even Canada.

Out of breath I reached the shelter of a long line of sand dunes, held fast by the tough marram grass. Thin mists of sand whined through the waving grasses, and I made for the shelter at the bottom of a deep dune. Here was a mass of driftwood thrown up by one of the winter gales. In the far north of Norway, on many days such as this, I would soon have had a fire blazing from the dry wood. Here I drew from my old leather rucksack my worn and battered kettle and an army heater, and despite missing the welcome flames of a fire, I soon had water boiling for some very hot tea.

Responding to the warmth from the drink and relaxing with the moan of the wind now high above my head, my thoughts went back over the centuries to the days when the hard strong men we call Vikings from Denmark and Norway had crept up the creeks of this lonely coast in their long ships.

As a small boy I had read myself to sleep by the light of a flickering candle with the stories of these men from the north coming over the sea in their flat-bottomed ships. They had plundered and killed men and women of the fishing villages they had discovered all along the coast, but eventually had begun to settle in this region of flatness.

The Danish raiders were the main attackers. Their first recorded appearance on our creeks was in 835, and after that raids came frequently in the ninth century. It is very easy to imagine these high-

'Sullen Winter had returned to this Coastal Region'

prowed, square-sailed long boats coming in with the flood-tide. They had very small keels, making it possible to sail over shallow water.

In 850 a group from Denmark wintered on our lonely and isolated coast, sharing the open space with the birds that would have used the mud-flats even then. It was in 866, however, that a large force came to seek homes here. They brought with them many skills, and a large number of the words we use today have their origins in the language of these 'men of the creeks', which is what the word 'Viking' really means.

Their long battles with Alfred the Great are set out in the exciting Anglo-Saxon Chronicle; there was a time when rule over part of the country was shared between the kings of Wessex and the rough kings from Scandinavia.

The stories of mountain ranges and of the great fiords of Norway from which came such men thrilled me. I could not know that one day I too would roam over such a landscape with my own sledge and reindeer, or watch the oystercatchers rising with the approaching autumn to fly back perhaps to the mud-flats over which I had just walked.

Other of my heroes came from the books of Sir Walter Scott, surely some of the finest adventure books that a young boy could ever read. Escaping with the explorers who had roamed the far corners of the earth, I listened with awe and rapture whilst a Major friend of my late Colonel father, who had himself spent many years in Africa, recounted to me some of his adventures in that then little known land of swamp and jungle. Borrowing every book we had from the library I read them all avidly. Today my library is an extensive one but still, much thumbed, lie before me the adventure-filled pages of *Tom Toms in the Night*, by the Italian explorer Attilo Gatti, and the more philosophical *The Gentle Art of Tramping* by Stephen Grahame. I also have a massive book called *The Vikings* which is a wonderful saga for any small boy who loves adventure.

Some of these books of mine, much read and much used, have accompanied me on all my trips both in England and abroad, but Grahame quotes one line that I have found to be true wherever my footsteps have taken me: 'Give me a companion of my way be it only to mention how the shadows lengthen as the sun declines.' So wrote Hazlitt and

'Pink-Feet Coming in near Holkham'
Above: 'Mostad, one of the Viking villages in north Norway'

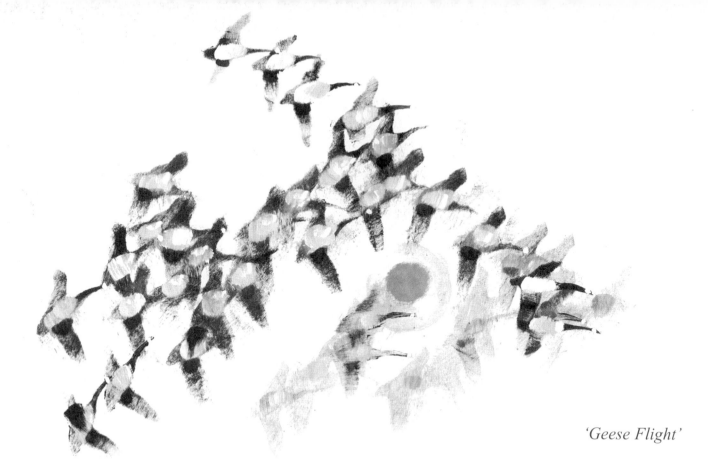

'Geese Flight'

how true is that sentence.

Within the lone traveller or walker wells up at sometime or other an almost overwhelming desire to express himself and his emotions to a companion: to talk of cabbages and kings, of the path ahead, of the way just left, of books, of people, of geese passing high overhead in a night sky, and of himself and his own emotions.

Some of my most memorable moments have been spent in the open, in company or proximity of those animals and humans who have taken the trail after dark. Or perhaps sitting round a smoky fire in a lonely cottage home where the fear of the

supernatural was still strong, and although fear was half hidden, it showed itself in many a glance and gesture. During my wartime adventures, the knock on the door at night was the most dreaded sound of all. Fear could chill the blood, and often I have felt the tingle of the scalp that comes from the terror of that sound. But even in these days of peace there are still many parts of the country where the darkness means a bolted door and a snarling welcome from the dog to any stranger who wishes to be guided on his way. The gleam of the yellow light or oil lamp can be far from friendly under these conditions, like the deceptive friendliness of the lighthouse beacon

'Ebbtide'

Brancaster marsh from Burnham Deepdale. A wide ranging view giving a commanding picture of the marshland here.

HUGH BRANDON-COX

attracting migrant birds to their doom.

I felt the cold creeping into my rather thin frame. A passing redshank yelled its alarm call as it saw me, and in the gloom swept over quickly on swift beating wings. My mind went back even further in time to the long gone age when Norfolk was still united to the continent. This great North Sea basin was once a land of forests and swamps and freshwater pools, before it was finally inundated with saltwater about 6400 BC. At several points

'Mussel Huts at Brancaster'

today on the Norfolk coast, at Titchwell for example, the trunks and stools of ancient trees can still be seen at low tide. Man has been around here for several thousand years, making a precarious living from the sea, and from small crofts in the early days as in the north of Norway.

The sky had now become almost grey-black and I arose stiff, to immediately feel the biting wind and the cold around my shoulders. It had become so dark that when I looked into the sky it was very clear and the burning points of Orion the Hunter and the Great Bear shone brightly, but the brightest of them all glowed the North Star. This has been the guiding light for generations, not only for fishermen and explorers and travellers, but also for countless millions of birds who have flown under this bright guide towards these desolate regions for their winter wild harvest.

My way back to Brancaster Staithe was guided by the many yellow lights coming from the houses of brick and flint with pantiles of red, strongly built to withstand the north winds. These are traditional Norfolk building materials, as is carstone which, when used with chalk, is known as 'clunch'. I gazed back over the way I had come and could hear gradually and then more urgently above the noise of the wind, the gurgle in the creeks as the tide began to sweep in to flood; such is its speed it is an unwise man who is out on these great mud-flats after the hour of darkness.

In our wanderings along this fascinating coastline we shall go from the Wash right round to Salthouse, exploring a series of fine nature reserves created by men and women of great dedication.

The influence of the tides and sea on this whole region has always been great. In 1565 it was noted for customs purposes, the names of Hunstanton,

'Brents in a Storm'
These are moments when the drama of the changing coast is seen at its best.

Hugh Brandon-Cox

Heacham, Wells, Thornham, Burnham, Brancaster, Blakeney, Wiveton, Cley and Salthouse, all of which were thriving ports. This was once one of England's busiest trading coastlines, but during the centuries a great deal of silting up and the movements of great sandbanks, with the withdrawal of the sea, have made the channels too drained and shallow to allow ships to come anywhere near most of these places. Wells, however, still has a number of vessels docking at the ancient waterside, as the channel is still deep enough to enable the passage of smaller cargo vessels.

I remember standing on the bank leading down to a fine area of pine trees and dunes at Wells, with the weather so cold that even the ebb-tide estuaries had a sheen of cracking ice on the shallow pools on the mud-flats. In the fields greylag geese could be glimpsed through the thin veil of mist. On the snow-covered banks by the channel a large flock of brent geese had gathered, their dark bodies contrasting greatly with the white scene around them. Large groups of coot, coming from the frozen lakes inland, wandered miserably over the snow, and a couple of grey herons huddled into their large wings to ward off the cold. All was so utterly different from the summer scene.

Wells is now the only port on this coastal strip with a suitable harbour and it has increased its business much of recent years. Cargoes such as animal feed, fish meal, potash and even potatoes are landed, and there has always been big business with whelks.

Agriculture and the sea were the reasons for Wells' existence, as was the case with many now quiet places such as Thornham. The fishermen of Wells made long trips in search of big catches, and the skilled

'Lowtide in the Creeks'

local shipwrights built sloops, schooners and brigs. It was indeed a hive of marine life. Sailmakers, ropemakers, carters, cargo handlers and merchants, blockmakers and chandlers all gathered in the local taverns. Wells in the early 1800s was the main port between King's Lynn and Yarmouth. Then more than 300 vessels a year docked at the quayside. It is rather ironic that it was the opening of the railway line in 1857 between Fakenham and Wells that aided the decline of the port.

'Pink-Feet Geese near Holkham' They come for the winter to the Norfolk coast in their thousands. *There are few flights of birds more impressive or thrilling than a huge mass of pink-feet with their far sounding calls.*

HUGH BRANDON-COX

Tough men have also manned the lifeboat here for many years and in 1880 eleven of the crew were drowned when on their way to help a grounded ship.

A great many visitors flock to the town each summer now because the charm of the past is still to be found. There is an attraction in watching a vessel unload its cargo which never seems to wane, and for the lovers of the sands and the dunes the long bank leading to the sea is well worth the walking.

'Blakeney Creek from Morston'

Please, however, I would urge you, never light fires under any circumstances, and if your valued companion happens to be a dog, please do keep it under strict control during the summer period when the birds are nesting. Birds such as oystercatchers, terns of all sorts, ringed plovers, redshanks and others, all have their nests on the ground between stones and among the dunes. They are so very easily disturbed by dogs so do keep your companion well by your side at all times.

'Wigeon in January on the Blakeney Marsh' A very lovely winter visitor with a chestnut head, yellow stripe and white belly. Coming from Scandinavia, Finland or Russia, their whistling calls are very distinctive and musical.

Chapter Two
The Vastness of the Wash

IT is a December day. The sun shines with a bleak and watery wintry brightness as I trudge along the shingle spit leading to the edge of the great sheet of mud and sand-flats we call the Wash. This is at the western end of our journey to the coast reserves, and is approached from the little town of Snettisham along the long track which leads eventually to the coast.

The Wash is the second largest area of inter-tidal land in the British Isles. When you stand on the edge of it on a day when the sun is glittering as now and it is ebb-tide again, the bright rays gleam on a vast expanse of mud that reflects the light with a silvery intensity. Sandbanks show just above the level of the mud, and the reserve comprises some 3650 acres, stretching into the distance so that the horizon meets the land in a shadowy misty edge that has no sharpness.

About twelve miles across this vast area is the Lincolnshire coast. From late July onwards into winter, huge flocks alight here. More than 300,000 birds make this paradise of mud their winter home, or a passing staging post on their way further south.

Birds of all species seem to have a common desire to band together during the winter months. I have been to the Arctic in the summer months and to the tundras where some of these geese and waders breed. There they space the distance between their nests, but in winter the flocks gather together in large numbers and begin to leave the dark Arctic areas, or the vast empty spaces of the tundra, to make a long migration taking them to several posts along the European coast. Eventually they reach an area such as the Wash, which is internationally known for the numbers that view it from above, and decide, 'Here is where we want to stay.' The mud is an absolute feast of small molluscs, crustaceans and worms. For instance, you can have up to 40,000 tiny snails, and a thousand or two of the rich lugworms in a square metre, apart from many many other sources of food that suit every type of bird that reaches here.

This lonely stretch was once the happy hunting ground of the wildfowlers and the men with their long punt guns. Now, of course, it has been taken over by the Royal Society for the Protection of

'Oystercatchers on a Winter Morning'
They gather in noisy chattering groups and are a very distinctive part of the huge winter bird population.

Birds who do a splendid job in maintaining the area as far as possible for the benefit of the birds and of the people who come to watch them. There are hides from which can be seen spectacular displays of birds coming together from vast distances with the flow of the tide.

As the tide approaches the shore so the waders are forced further and further inwards and viewers from the hides are rewarded with a rare variety of flashing wings. There are knot and dunlin, the large pied black-and-white figures of the oystercatchers with their yelping cries, together with bar-tailed godwits, turnstones, curlew, ringed plovers, grey plovers, redshanks, and the delightful little sanderlings. These seem to be like toy mechanical birds running around on fast moving dark legs. As they fly they assume the appearance of tiny silver fish in large numbers, disappearing and appearing as though in a flash, all at once. Many other rare and shy birds add variety to this scene of wild winter movement and noise.

You will not, of course, see them all at one time, don't expect that; but with good eyesight and a pair of binoculars you should have a most enjoyable and memorable time at this spot, whether the wind is blowing keenly in your face as it is today into mine, or the sun is shining warmly on a still day and conditions feel ideal.

I have always had a great affection for oystercatchers. They are bold pied black-and-white birds with a strong long orange beak and pink legs, and if you are reading this in the summer time you will undoubtedly have seen several pairs of them. If you have, by mischance, come near to any of their

'Oystercatchers near Morston'

nests in the sand or dunes, you will have heard a 'kleeping' alarm call warning you away from their eggs or young.

As I stand gazing into the wind, watching these large birds, my mind goes back to the far north of Norway. One particular spot, the little old deserted village of Mostad, I must tell you about because it was once the scene of such bustling fishing life and wild beauty that I would love to go there once more

'Pink-Feet Geese' A wonderful sight on a fine day.
The whole time they are passing overhead their calls reach down to give a thrilling effect to the whole scene.

to savour real lonely wildness. It was an evening in August and the candle flame spluttered fitfully whilst the shadows danced on the wooden walls of the old school-house at the very edge of the sea in this small, now deserted, village in north Norway. The building, on its base of rocks, groaned and creaked as the shrieking wind howled in from the sea. Above us the bell clanged in the storm. The wind was mixed with dirty grey salt spray as it struck hard against the window panes.

Across the wide and stormy bay, very similar in some ways to this big Wash, the mountains were obscured by thick scudding clouds swirling down almost to the level of the angry white-topped waves. The sense of isolation was strong. Around the school-house were the boarded-up shells of the wooden homes once filled with fishing families. This old room we were in had once resounded with the noise of children. Mostad, the village under the great cliff, now lived

on its memories, inhabited by one lonely old man and his wife, and the teeming multitudes of sea birds that swept restlessly round the cliffs all summer.

The force of the late summer gale, so common in this region above the Arctic Circle, affected the senses so that after a while we sat as if in a trance while the gloom in the small room grew deeper where the candle light did not reach.

Ulla Maija, my young Finnish wife, who could survive in almost any primitive conditions, shook herself from her reverie and turned to place more driftwood on the old black stove. In the oven her rye bread was rising, turning golden brown. When the door was opened for a moment, the room filled with the strong sour smell of the bread. Wood for the fire had been gathered from the rocks on the tide edge. The strength of the draught made the grey wood draw in fierce flames of bright yellow. The long days and nights of eternal light in the period of

'Pink-Feet Geese'

'Brents over the Burnham Overy Sky'
Typical of blustery days on the coast.

Hugh Branson Cox

the midnight sun were over. Very soon the days would pass from their continual summer lightness to the pale twilight of winter. Sunless would come the long dark days that are almost indistinguishable from the night.

The storm slowly abated, leaving our world damp and cold in the wake of the winds. Thick vegetation rose high on the sides of the cliffs, enriched with a welcome harvest of delicious blueberries and the large golden cloudberries. Over the slopes the willow grouse were on fast beating wings, calling restlessly, 'go back, go back'. The old birds warned us constantly when we came too close to their large families of rapidly growing young, hiding between the rocks by the side of the rainwater streams. Around us also called the oystercatchers, yelping and kleeping as soon as they saw us. They were unused to human company in this part of the world where they had the whole environment to themselves all summer. Now the thick fog returned to swirl around the tops of the mountains. It was nearly time for us to leave – so too for the oystercatchers.

So one afternoon shortly after this the whole flock of the oystercatchers had gathered together.

'Good Sailing near Morston'

Suddenly, as if by command, they took off – flying straight into the sun which was setting behind the high cliff rocks. We knew then that this summer of a million wings was over. These very birds that we were watching taking off so effortlessly into the air might by some miracle of migration arrive in the Wash where I stand gazing today. Even more wonderful, some of the very birds that I am looking at might have been those that we had watched and heard around that deserted old village in the far north.

I shook myself from my thoughts because the wind was shrieking into my ears once more reminding me that I was getting very cold. Turning, I walked back to the beginning of the reserve, resolving to come back at night to see the huge flocks of pink-feet geese that come to this part of the Wash and the surrounding fields for the winter months. You can hear them in the distance sometimes as they drop down on to the muddy earth that has been rich with sugar-beet and potatoes, and now winter wheat showing. They feed on these and seem to enjoy their diet immensely. But I wanted to see if it was possible to have a glimpse and hear the sound of a fresh migrating flock as they arrive by night.

'Brent Flight near Scolt Head'

Hugh Brandon-Cox

So with the approaching tide and with the darkness closing in around me, I returned to this long shingle spit. The wind had died down considerably, giving me the chance to see again the velvet night sky with stars showing brightly. I settled myself in the shelter of a large clump of marram grass and prepared to wait. Warmly clad, I had a flask of hot drink with me. I had not been sitting long when away in the far distance I heard a faint, faint sound I can only describe as exactly resembling a pack of baying hounds on the scent. It was, to be sure, a huge flock of pink feet coming in for the first time to drop down on to the water. There they would remain for the rest of the night.

These birds keep in touch with each other as they fly through the darkness. For me, gazing at the great galaxy of stars, there is a feeling of utter isolation from the massive problems of humanity. The calls of the geese reach down faintly at first. Then they increase to a sound that is unlike any other one will hear. It is anxious; the calling of one to another to bring comfort that the whole great flock is moving together.

I feel the lonely thrill of it all in my spine and as the sound gradually recedes into the black-blue distance so the night air on the edge of the mud-flats seems to be ever colder. I am vividly reminded of a night on a lonely spit of land in the lower Arctic, waiting for the reindeer to come down from the heights for transport over to a small island for the summer grazing. It was so cold, without any tent, that the morning light found me almost frozen. My Lapp friend, who had a small Lapp tent, soon had a fierce blaze from burning heather and with a very hot drink I eventually thawed a little.

A thin streak of pale dawn light showed in the east where I sat after the geese had disappeared. This would be the first time that this particular flock had arrived here. Normally as soon as the daylight came they would be up and finding the fields, probably the same fields where they had fed the previous winter. This is one of the fantastic features of migration travel. Birds will return to the same area and some even, as we know with swallows, to the same building as they have known the previous summer.

Making my way back from the Snettisham Point, I was drawn to the light reflected back from the big shingle pits now filled with brackish water. These attract up to a third of all the birds that feed on the Wash at the flood of the tide. There they gather in big flocks. These manmade lagoons were created shortly after the First World War, and at that time they were used for commercial extraction of the shingle. But then this was halted by the great flood of 1953 and now, of course, they are managed by the RSPB. Any shingle movement is merely to create more suitable banks

'Badgers' Not the birds but one of Norfolk's most attractive but secretive creatures, the badger. We have a great many sets in the coastal rural areas.

and islands for the birds to rest in safety before resuming their quest for food.

You know, one of the geese you must watch for all along the coast, and you will see them here, are the brents. The Norfolk heritage strip has known them for many years. They are smallish plumpish geese, and many thousands come to this part of the coast for the winter. You will see them rising up as I did at Snettisham Point. They give the impression of an all-black appearance as they fly. Really they have a dark grey belly, a black neck with a small patch of white and a very clearly showing white rump. When they fly they have a very distinctive call: 'ronk, ronk, ronk'. The sound reaches down as they are disturbed at their feeding and take to the air in a wheeling flight. At one time their numbers had declined drastically because of the near elimination of the eel-grass on which they fed. But today, because of improved conditions in recent years and because they are not shot at by wildfowlers, their numbers have increased immensely and they are one of the real winter delights. Several hundred feed

BADGERS

HUGH BRANDON-COX

on the reserve in late winter, and big groups of the large and very boldly coloured shelduck make the Wash their resting place during the moult.

There were many of the bright orange berries of the sea buckthorn still hard on the thorny bushes when I watched the birds of the pools, but they would soon be snapped up by migrants from Norway.

The watchers who make for the hides by the pools may well have a good sighting of such birds as little grebe, gadwall, tufted duck, many mallard, the lovely whistling wigeon, coot, shoveler, scaup, great crested grebe, the delightful small teal, mergansers, and even the long-tailed duck and smew.

You may catch a sight of immature eider duck, with whom I had a long association in north Norway, and even flocks of common scoters, but be highly delighted with whatever birds you see, because all have an individual charm and appeal that make their watching so rewarding.

If you are visiting the reserve during the breeding season, watch out for the ringed plovers, redshanks and oystercatchers, and also the colony of common terns, the sea swallows of the coast, that nest on the small islands in the pools.

The Wash also has the largest group of common

seals, between 5000 and 7000, ar[...] coasts. They have their pups in lat[...] young can swim from birth, unlike th[...] Pelt hunting was stopped in 1973. seen near the reserves as they are be[...] the deeper waters in the middle of the Wash. The probably find most of their food outside this big region, being good long-distance swimmers.

Perhaps the most interesting of the very many plants of the saltmarsh and seashore here are the big yellow-horned poppies, sea-kale, and at the top of the beach, the white flowers of the sea-campion, the yellow birdsfoot trefoil, and

'Oystercatchers at Dusk'

the very attractive blue vipers bugloss. There is so much to appeal to the lover of this windswept area where the sky is indeed very much an ever-changing part of the daily pattern of life.

28

'Solitude' An example of how the solitude of this often seen but lonely bird can have a deep emotional appeal. I painted this along the coast just after the tragic death of my young Finnish wife.

Hugh Brandon-Cox

Chapter Three

The Long Heritage Coastline

YOU may be sitting at the base of the multicoloured cliffs at Hunstanton, from the top of which the Lincolnshire coast can be seen over the Wash. The cliffs are a mixture of layers of white chalk, red limestone, and carstone, and are a hunting ground for fossil collectors. It is summer. The bitter winds of winter have gone and you are enjoying a peaceful, relaxed and somewhat more old-fashioned holiday. This is how towns like Hunstanton gained such popularity in the Victorian era, with the advent of the railway in the 1860s. Formerly I lived in Cambridge and remember very well making such train journeys from that city to Hunstanton for what I considered splendid outings. One winter day after such an excursion, and with film camera and tripod, I trudged along to the end of the stone sea-defence wall, coming to the sands where at low tide large beds of mussels appear. These are eaten and enjoyed by the oystercatchers, and around the dark shells that day were a group kleeping away as ever, plunging their strong bills into the mussels to get at the soft yellowish flesh inside.

In my excitement to try to film them and my desire to come ever closer I had not noticed the rapidly approaching flood-tide. Suddenly I found myself standing on a raised sandbank, realising I was being marooned. The swift flow was now all around me and becoming much deeper every moment. Gazing around in dismay at the very cold water, the only sign of life appeared to be a distant horse and cart, used to gather shellfood, going out across the sandbanks at low tide. The two men in the cart saw my plight and trundled over towards me. One of the men in very long rubber boots got out, splashed through the water, hoisted me on to his back with my camera and tripod, and took me back to the cart. These two men, so typical of the good-humoured folk who earn a living from the sea, got me back to dry land and made a joke about the whole adventure.

I am sure that evening in their local pub my situation became the subject of a deal of ribald humour. I was reminded of a bitter day in north Norway when the turf roof of my small cabin by the sea lost a good portion of the covering in a massive night of wind. The following morning two young fishermen I knew, seeing my plight, came to my aid with a large piece of sailcloth. This they worked

HUGH BRANDON-Cox

with a will to fix so that I could at least be dry, even if the interior of the cabin was a dismal place in such weather. Wind and storms are only known by the people who really have to face them in villages and groups on the edge of the sea that can be a bitter and savage foe at such times.

In recent years we have had several such severe tides, aided by strong winds, which have severely tested the sea-defences. Grazing land, long ago reclaimed from the sea, is then flooded leaving a thick salt deposit, and the villages that are low-lying also suffer from the swelling surging water. It is a constant battle to decide where and how much can be spent on holding back the sea when it shows a face of white fury.

This little episode was some years ago, but if you are interested in birds, you can still see, even in summer time, the mussel beds with oystercatchers gathered there making a noisy and distinctive showing in their black and white plumage.

Moving up from Hunstanton, with its old-fashioned delights and charm, you enter a realm of great beauty and excitement on what is now known as the Heritage Coast. Between Holme and Salthouse lie 25 miles of sea-covered saltmarshes, shingle spits, sand dunes, inter-tidal bays and lagoons, with their ever-changing movements of birds both summer and winter. Designated an area of outstanding natural beauty and protected, there are along this whole length important nature reserves created through the dedication of the RSPB, the National Trust or the Norfolk Wildlife Trust.

The great saltmarshes are unique in their composition. A squelching delight at any time of the year, they have their soft ever-changing colouring and a mass of tough plant life. Plants that exist in this watery region can survive being covered twice a day. So much variety will make you want to study them closer. Deeply cut creeks and riverlets wind and snake through these marshes, making them difficult at times to cross. It is certainly a muddy game, but worth it for the exhilaration of being in the midst of the strong tang of the sea. When the tide sweeps in, the mud assumes a silver sheen and a strong odour, and on the banks are plants you will see nowhere else. The atmosphere has a quality of being miles from the worries and stresses of ordinary town life.

Whether it is summer or winter saltmarshes are some of the most fascinating places to wander. You are never really alone, because even when humans are not seen, there is always a residue of bird life, with the redshanks ready to cry in alarm at your intrusion, just to show that they are there, as vigilant as ever.

On a bright clear day one of the charms of this area is to listen to the song of a skylark high above.

'Early May'
The coastal fields are filled with bright yellow rape.

HUGH BRANDON-COX

You need only stand and gaze into the wide sky and listen to this small bird delighting in its freedom in a world little disturbed by man, and very rightly so.

Saltmarshes are formed through the centuries by a mixture of silt, clay and sand mixing together to

Homeward on a Winter's Afternoon

form a muddy bed that can be colonised by a host of sea-tolerant plants. There are areas where a beautiful soft grey paints large spaces. When you examine these plants and drag your fingers through the sea southernwood, you scent an aromatic fragrance. Plants such as scrubby sea-blite, sea-purslain, sea-plantain, sea-arrow grass, sea-sandwort, sea-asters and strong cord grass lend some of their special qualities of survival to the saltmarshes. Perhaps the one that glows the most is the lovely sea-lavender, fading into the distance as far as the eye can see during its summer time of blooming.

Of course a lot of these deep channels need a bridge. You will find many very old planks have been thrown across narrow parts, as walkers have scrambled over them in the past. Sometimes you will see a pair of the worm-diggers going out, clad in their very long sea boots, with pails and forks. They stand out on the glittering mud of the flats as they dig for the lug-worms, which can produce quite a fair income as they are in such great demand, and have been for many years.

If you squelch through the mud at the right time of the year, when the samphire or glasswort comes into bloom, you will likely see a host of people with buckets picking what looks like small succulent green cactus plants. It has been said, quite seriously, that, 'no one has lived until they have eaten samphire for supper off a saltmarsh'. This sounds a bit of an exaggeration but it is a tasty, salty dish. You boil the shoots for five minutes, then put plenty of butter on them, drawing the stems through the teeth with your fingers, leaving nothing but the

HUGH BRANDON-COX

The Rural Life we Would Like to Preserve for the Future. One of my Favourite small paintings.'

skeleton and root behind. Greatly prized in the Norfolk area, they have been growing there in the mud for very many generations.

Great Britain is such a minute spot on the world map, but we have reserves and these great mud-flats of such international importance to wildlife which can appear out of all proportion to the size of our small island. But leaving the saltmarshes and the flats for a moment; the narrow lanes of the countryside just inland from the coast are as fascinating in their own way as any big nature reserve.

For years as a boy, and now as an ageing wanderer, I have walked the muddy fields that surround this area. Nothing perhaps is more evocative than the short time when the sun is just sinking behind the horizon, and the rooks are swooping down in a noisy swarming flock to feed in the fields. It is a rural scene that changes but little through the years, although gone today are the small ragged boys with their rattles once used to scare the rooks from the field; their places have been taken by very unpleasant sounding alarm machines. The impression of these fields close to the shore, now they have grown to immense size, is still of lonely isolation for the worker in his tractor.

In the north of Norfolk, around the Brancaster area for example, the ploughlands can disappear into the distance and the sound of the machine is only faintly heard. As you travel close to them on the narrow lanes it seems as though they are devoid of all human life. Farm cottages no longer stand where once they must have done. Now the emergence of immense and complicated farm machines means that the work that through the year had occupied a large army of farm workers can now be done by two or three men.

How the farming pattern has changed in the last hundred years. Old photographs show, and I can remember them myself too, colourful parties of men, wives and children gathered in their fields at harvest time, and all playing their vital role in the farming scene.

We know labour had been cheap and plentiful, and living conditions primitive, but at least the families helped each other through all adversities and in sickness. There was, of course, no money from any government to support them. I was

'March Afternoon, North Norfolk'
How we like to think of the charm of rural Norfolk.

reminded of the same fact when living with the Lapps in north Norway. We had huge swampy areas producing wild berries that needed to be gathered in for winter and the Lapps themselves, like the old farm workers of north Norfolk from the past, have always been ready to support each other at all times and in difficult circumstances.

Whilst we are in these country lanes, muddy as they still are when the sugar-beet is being harvested, we can remember that at the beginning of the 18th century much of this land was even then being farmed in big open fields. It was Thomas Coke of Holkham who adopted the idea of the Norfolk four-course crop rotation, applied it to his home farms and imposed it on all his tenants.

This rotation gave much greater yields and reduced pests and disease, but the land had to be enclosed to keep livestock from the crops. Hedges and trees were planted and the open fields swept away in a surge of enthusiasm for the Enclosures.

One of the best husbanded areas of farm land in the country is an apt description of Norfolk. Good rich soils growing fine crops of wheat, barley, oats, oilseed rape, potatoes and above all, perhaps, sugar-beet, have given this county a series of very productive farms. There has been a definite and welcome lack of enthusiasm in the past few years for dragging out the long lines of thick hedgerows that were once made for the Enclosures. Thankfully, this trend for pulling up the old hedges has been reversed, and now farmers are even planting lines of hedgerows for future years.

The last 100 years have seen a dramatic change in the social habits of country and town people. The coming of the motor-car and the railways made such an immense and significant difference to this coastal area. Before then, farming had known habitual declines and rises in income, and there was a growing shortage of workers from the 1850s. Norfolk had been very slow to adapt to changing technology. The farmers resisted the use of the excellent threshing machines until late in the century, although other counties had been ready to adopt them.

The grain from these very productive fields had to be carefully stored and the early 1800s was the period when most of the fine old flint and brick barns of north Norfolk were built. They were made to last through the centuries, and I feel that far too many have been converted to private homes. They were never designed for such a purpose. The granaries with their massive doors were usually kept locked, as the grain was the most valuable stored product of the farm.

'Avocet Evening'
By kind permission of Michael Barnwell

Hugh Brandon-Cox

Avocet Evening

The long story behind the great fields of north Norfolk is full of drama, change and varied produce. For every farm there had to exist craftsmen of all types, necessary to maintain the pattern of rural life. Wheelwrights, carpenters, blacksmiths, wagon makers, thatchers, shepherds, good ploughmen, who cared for the horses, and skilled farm general workers and hedge-layers: all had a vital role at every month of the year.

In winter on the desolate saltings and sand dunes the sounds of the exploding punt guns were part of the natural scheme of life.

All this has really changed so very rapidly over the past few decades. Now every village has its quota of holiday homes. The old cottages have been brightly repaired to good advantage, with a complete facelift to the whole area in so many ways. The protection societies for the countryside and wildlife have all emerged during the last hundred years. Now in every village there are many more people from far away who would never have been found so distant from their roots in the past. A day's outing by cart to the seaside was once valued as the annual holiday for so many in the villages and small towns, but what a contrast it is today!

The English have always had rather a romantic notion of living or retiring to a home close to the sea. Because of this the population of these northern

'Winter at Burham Norton'

'A Rural Autumn Scene, North Norfolk'

HUGH BRANDON-COX

villages along the coastal strip of Norfolk has grown immensely over the past years. On the outskirts of each village, new houses and estates have mushroomed and it is often regrettable that these ancient hamlets and villages, with their historical and charming old flint churches and nucleus of ancient homes, are being invaded by so many new properties.

That is why this Heritage Coast, this dramatic coastline from Holme round the bulge of Norfolk, is of such ever-growing importance. This windswept area of massive fields, invading geese, shifting sand, saltmarshes and freedom of flight for so many migrating birds, is also an oasis of freedom of thought and movement for the person who longs to escape from the crowded streets of city life. Thankfully, we can hope that this area is preserved now for the future, and will not be more disturbed than it is already.

The village of Holme-next-the-Sea makes quite an impression, consisting mostly of chalk, clunch, brick and flint walls and cottages. At the end of these is the Holme Dunes Nature Reserve. It is, and this is a personal feeling, one of the wildest and most exhilarating stretches of the coast.

The sand dunes, heavily coated with tough marram grass, are raised above the magnificent vista of lonely shoreline stretching into the far distance. On a cold January morning I had the huge cloud-filled skyline, and the sound of the breaking waves of a receding tide, to myself. On the edge of the waves ran and flew dunlin and sanderlings, whilst oystercatchers kept a watch on the wet sand as I moved along towards them. This is an English wilderness at its best.

In March come the first spring migrants: the chiffchaffs and wheatears; and later in May fly in the flycatchers, wood warblers, redstarts, and even perhaps a bluethroat. Marsh and Montague's harriers, ospreys and hobbies can be looked for, whilst a large variety of birds breed on the grazing marshes. Hides give excellent views of the lovely delicate black-and-white avocets which breed in the pools.

Holme reserve is worthy of a visit at any time of year. It was near here, in Holme Bay, that a startling discovery was made back in 1998. A Bronze Age timber circle, known locally as Seahenge, emerged from the peat, sand and mud to capture the imagination of the world's media. The circle, eventually discovered to be over 4000 years old, was one of the most important archaeological discoveries to have occurred in Norfolk during the 20th century; it was certainly one of the most controversial. Its excavation was opposed by many of the local residents and, along with protesters from the Druid orders, they managed to start an on-going debate that received international media coverage. Despite this the circle was eventually excavated and removed to the specialist ancient timber facility at Flag Fen near Peterborough where it remains to this day.

'Old Norfolk Barn near Walsingham'
So many of these fine old barns, so essential formerly to the running of the farms, have been converted to homes.

HUGH BRANDON-COX

Chapter Four

Titchwell, Brancaster and The Burnhams

ONLY 350 years ago this whole area of the Norfolk coast was a seldom visited plain of sand dunes and saltmarsh. It is impressive to think how this wilderness has been developed to produce not only agricultural land but also fine nature reserves.

Between Thornham and Titchwell villages on the main coastal road is Titchwell Nature Reserve. A track leads to the car park, and a site of which the RSPB can be proud indeed.

This is one of the regions where the marsh was reclaimed for agricultural use, but has since reverted to saltmarsh. Sea walls were built in the 1780s, and root crops and beef were produced on the enclosed land for nearly 150 years. The storms that battered the walls in January 1953 destroyed a great deal of the northern sea defences. The unchecked waves flooded over fields which gradually reverted back to saltmarsh.

It was in the 1970s that the RSPB realised the potential of this area. When the reserve was in its infancy, tides flooded the saltmarsh and most of the reed-beds during the summer thus stopping any ground-nesting birds from breeding. To encourage more birds, part of the saltmarsh and the reed-beds were protected from the tides by the building of a large sea wall. Using a system of sluices to control water levels, the enclosed land is managed as freshwater reed-bed, freshwater marsh and brackish marsh. A raised walk starts from the information centre, and on the left-hand side are the marshes, containing lovely spreads of sea-lavender, which have never been reclaimed. Tides have deposited fine layers of silt there, and the marsh level has gradually risen. Only about ten per cent of the tides now flood the marsh, and plants such as the sea-lavender, sea-pink, sea-purslain, sea-arrow grass and saltmarsh grasses thrive. This means that birds such as partridges, redshanks, mallards, skylarks, meadow pipits and even reed buntings can now nest there. Plants that provide food for flocks of brent geese in winter also grow well, and skylarks, greenfinches and even goldfinches and twites feed there. The lovely, and quite rare, hen harriers, and short-eared owls are also regular winter visitors.

On the right-hand side as you walk down this path the flooded marshlands provide a source of much interest. On the freshwater marsh the shallow

'Brents Coming in at Titchwell'
One can spend a long time at this remarkable reserve, with so much to study

HUGH BRANDON-COX

'Overy Staithe from Burnham Norton'

flooding has converted the original saltmarsh vegetation into a layer of organic matter rich in aquatic life, whilst the brackish marsh is kept flooded for most of the year to prevent vegetation growth on the low islands. This results in an open area of mud and shallow water. Black-headed gulls, oystercatchers and Canada geese nest in this area.

Titchwell's most prized resident is of course the avocet. These first came to breed here in 1984 and by 1988 the population had exceeded 40 pairs, making Titchwell one of Britain's largest breeding colonies. Now the population is more usually about 30 pairs.

In the summer that charming little visitor from Africa, the reed warbler, may be found with its suspended nest. I have always delighted in trying to watch and film these small birds, but unfortunately for them, they are prey to the cuckoo which lays its egg in their reed-held nest. The foster parents feed and rear a chick that grows several times larger than themselves! You may also find the colourful bearded tits nesting at the base of the reed-beds, among many other birds that are dwellers in the thick reeds where they feel safe and find their food. In autumn the water levels are lowered so that waders can eat in the shallows.

'Canada Geese Coming In'

A very large handsome goose that has taken well to the coastal regions. Many remain to breed in small lakes and pools.

HUGH BRANDON-COX

At the end of this path opens out an expanse of sand and shingle where are the remains of what was once a giant forest, long before the sea drowned the land. Some of the stumps of ancient oaks still protrude from the sand.

Below the dunes and the beach is the foreshore, a wide sweep of slippery grey clay overlaid with various depths of sand. All this is covered by the tides every day. If you turn to the right the beach widens out into a large space where common terns, oystercatchers and ringed plovers nest in the early summer. All these ground-nesting birds are easily disturbed – by people or horses – and it is very easy to destroy their eggs.

'March Morning'

In the autumn and winter, as I well know, this shoreline is visited by large numbers of waders. At times there may be 30,000 birds, mainly knots, the distinctive bar-tailed godwits, oystercatchers, and lesser numbers of ringed and grey plovers, sanderlings and turnstones.

There is also a fascinating walk if you turn left, and among the shingle and sand dunes ringed plovers and oystercatchers have their nests. If you are too near they will rise and sweep round and round, with their strident alarm call to warn you off.

This is a reserve that summer and winter is fascinating whatever the weather. It owes much of its attraction to its dedicated warden and the helpers who assist in patrolling the reserve especially in summer. They are to be congratulated on their valuable work and also for the information centre. With its excellent descriptions of the habitats of birds and plants, it is certainly a credit to a reserve that you should not miss.

Leaving Titchwell and going a little further along this coastal road, you come to Brancaster, which has been described as the gateway to Nelson country, and to the Burnhams. There is a long coastal walk which you could start at Holme, and proceed to discover the lure of both the saltmarshes on one hand, and the fields and countryside on the other, right to the end of this Heritage Coast if you delight in long-distance walking.

Brancaster Staithe on a cold winter's day is a far different sight to the summer scene. Then sailing boats of every type fill the channel with multicoloured sails and all is bustle and activity. This staithe once had a regular sea trade in coal and grain, and in 1841 six master mariners are said to have lived here. Before that the staithe is said to have had one of the largest malt houses in the country. Now, of course, the village is almost hemmed in by saltings, and is a good watery leisure centre.

'Old Mussel Huts at Brancaster Staithe' A place that one has to visit to appreciate the great appeal of the ebbtide mud-flats, the birds, and the background of Scolt Head. The finest mussels are to be found here.

HUGH BRANDON COX

The National Trust has been established on the north Norfolk coast since 1912 and its initiative has brought in a number of most welcome partners, so that by far the greater part of the coast between Hunstanton and Sheringham is now managed for the preservation of its exceptional scientific interest. Brancaster Staithe is the centre of the western section, and the Brancaster Millennium Activity Centre in the Dial House is an education centre fully equipped to be enjoyed by schools and groups from all over the country learning

'Burnham Overy Mill'

about the coast and environmental sustainability. The centre was opened in 2000 and from there you may embark for Scolt Head island, 1,620 acres of sand dune, saltmarsh, ever-changing shingle ridge and foreshore, with a ternery (in which sandwich terns are particularly abundant) at its western end. There is no access to the ternery during the breeding season in May, June and July.

The island can be reached over the mud-flats at low water, but only by those who really know the route. The beach is little frequented and makes a good walk for a beachcomber. The island was acquired in 1927, but it was not until 40 years later that the 2,220 acres of Brancaster marshes, on the mainland opposite, were bought, adding greatly to the value of this lovely place.

As a small boy I had a much-read book about Scolt Head written by a couple who had spent a year there studying the nature. To me it all sounded terribly remote and romantic. Of course, it is not as I dreamt as a boy, but go over there if you can in summer, and you will enjoy another bracing day.

Recently on a very wild and windy day I was talking to one of the men who have the arduous, and in winter very cold, work of mussel farming. They have their little individual sheds, and through the ages mussels have provided a living for many families along the coast. Now, I was told, he had been compelled to spend £13,000 on new tanks in which the mussels had to be more thoroughly cleansed than ever before. Young mussels, which are called seeds, are collected from breeding grounds in the Wash, and then transplanted in 'leys' in the Brancaster creeks, to be left for two or three years to grow. They are

In a wonderful period when the lonely world of the long coastal flats is at its best, with birds far into the distance

Hugh Brandon-Cox

'Viking long boats coming into the Norfolk creeks.'

then sorted, riddled, and washed overnight in what used to be ordinary pools of water. The new regulations mean they must be cleaned in these special expensive tanks. Always in great demand, mussels are sent to London, and many more go up to the Midlands.

Hardy walkers leave Brancaster Staithe behind on the coastal path. This is now an ever-changing world of sea birds, creeks, sky, and wind. Soon you are in a lonely domain of your own, walking towards Burnham Norton. It appears in the distance across windswept Norton marsh.

You also have a distant view of Burnham Overy Mill, with its black framework and white sails. It is quite a landmark when you stand on the marshy edge of Burnham Norton. The village is charming with traditional flint and brick and carstone buildings, maintaining its air of being

unconnected with the present coastal road. Right on the very edge of the marsh, it was not always in such an isolated position. Certainly worth a visit is the old church of Burnham Norton, some distance away from the village. In fact it is only a short distance from Burnham Market, on a ridge overlooking the sea. The romantic fiction surrounding the round-towered churches of East Anglia suggests that these towers were originally free standing and erected as strong retreats or look-out posts by the Saxons against the Vikings. On the sighting of a raiding party, women and children and their valuables would all be taken to the narrow opening in the tower about 30 feet above the ground, where they could be safe from attack. The facts, however, do not support this theory. The Vikings did make raids, as I have said before, from about 870, but these ended when King Canute took the throne in 1016. The earliest remaining church buildings in Norfolk date, however, from about 1030. It is a shame to spoil such a story, because the tower itself suggests such a safe refuge.

The village of Burnham Norton once probably clustered all round this lovely Norman church but eventually moved to the edge of the marshes. It was due, some think, to the sweeping ravages of the Black Death in 1364, with other causes such as the depopulation due to Tudor sheep farming. In any case now it stands alone, facing the cold wind century after century, as solid as in the days when the fine craftsmen built it.

'Always there can be found a quiet corner to be alone. This is at Burnham Overy Staithe.'

HUGH BRANDON-COX

Following the main coastal road you come to the little harbour of Burnham Overy Staithe. The quay here is the essence of the staithe which is a pleasant village with many moored boats in summer. Formerly another flourishing port, it was able to make the transition to an agricultural village with the coming of the railway. You have a hint here of Horatio Nelson in the local pub which is called 'The Hero', and we are now beginning to move into the essential Nelson country. Once there were seven Burnham villages, though only five properly survive today: Burnham Deepdale, Burnham Norton, Burnham Market, Burnham Overy and Burnham Thorpe.

Horatio Nelson was born at Burnham Thorpe in 1758, either in what was the old rectory or near it. His father, who was not a rich man, was Rector. Horatio was the sixth of eleven children, and the family lived near the fast-flowing little river Burn, from which the seven Burnhams took their name.

His early years were spent in one of those cold old rectories, bleak and dismal in winter and almost within sound of the sea. Early years were saddened by the death of his mother when he was only nine. The Rector had great difficulty in caring for his large family, and in spite of his efforts all the children tried to find work for themselves at the earliest possible age.

'Geese Flying over Old Farm at Burnham Norton'

'Evening Flight'
There is always a wild beauty when geese or duck take off in the dusk of evening.

Hugh BRANDON-fox

Nelson, despite being a very frail boy, at the age of twelve reported to join his uncle's ship, the *Raisonable*. It was in those days a terribly hard life, and it is hard for me to understand its appeal. In any case Horatio survived very well. He also managed somehow to find time to get married and seven years later returned to Burnham Market for a period of frustrating semi-retirement. His poor young wife

'Road to Burnham Thorpe'

Fanny, who had been used to the warmth of the West Indies, must have found the conditions terribly cold and miserable at Burnham Thorpe in the winter and took to her bed for long periods with various colds and coughs.

Nelson continued his naval service later and went on to become quite a hero at a young age. He also commenced a dramatic love affair with Lady Emma Hamilton, the wife of Sir William, British Ambassador at the court of the King of Naples. He lost the sight of one eye at the siege of Calvi, and he also lost his right arm at Tenerife. Eventually he went on a grand tour with the Hamiltons, through Europe and around Great Britain. And this was in spite of his continuing love affair with Emma. The forlorn figure in this story was poor Frances, who was broken-hearted by Nelson's rejection of her.

We all know from our school days of the famous victory at Trafalgar, and the tragic manner that Nelson's life ended there. His last words were considered to be, 'Thank God I have done my duty.' Visit Burnham Thorpe church. It is another wonderfully strong and fascinating example of Norman building, with massive stone pillars running down each side of the aisles. Absorbing the atmosphere in the church and seeing the font where young Nelson was baptised, it is easy to feel close to this historical drama.

Before leaving this region of sweeping views and history-filled villages, do pay a visit to Burnham Market. An elegant, mostly Georgian, small town around an extensive green, the number of people there on any day, summer or winter, always seems to me quite remarkable. A typical example of an English town that any visitor from abroad should be shown, for its variety of genteel buildings and general air of prosperity.

'Corner of Burnham Overy Staithe'
An extremely busy corner all the summer months.

Hugh Brandon-Cox

Chapter Five

Holkham and onwards to Morston, Blakeney, Cley and Salthouse

HOLKHAM BAY is a wonderful region for getting mud on your boots. The tide recedes to a great distance allowing several miles of wet sand walking, with a backcloth of the pines called the Holkham meals, planted to stop the dunes eroding further into the land. There has been a tremendous amount of silting through the years, but it now enables the visitor to enjoy a most spacious, windswept and fascinating area.

You will probably have visited nearby Holkham Hall, which has been described as a most perfect example of a great house built in the Palladian style. Holkham was the product of the great wealth of the Coke family. They are an example of many who rose to wealth and greatness through the upheaval which followed the Reformation. The Hall itself stands in magnificent grounds.

By the way, after a visit to the great Holkham bay, which you will find tremendously invigorating, return via Lady Anne's Drive and stop for a while at the Victoria Hotel. Built in 1838, the year after Queen Victoria's accession to the throne, this hotel, with its Oriental style and furniture from India, offers an elegant glimpse into her vast Empire.

Good food, excellent wine, and the most welcoming staff will make for relaxed enjoyment of every moment. It is one of my favourite contrasts to the rigours of the mud-flats and the saltmarshes.

Going further along the coast road we come to the village of Stiffkey, which is nearly all comprised of flint houses. Running behind the village is the little river Stiffkey.

Both the coastal road and the long-distance path now head for what was once the small port of Morston. There is still a fairly good deep channel here at high tide, and more and more popular is the trip over to Blakeney Point, which can be seen from Morston. This important nature reserve, which is really at the end of a continuous ridge of shingle, was given to the National Trust in 1912, and became one of the first reserves established in Norfolk. An old lifeboat house among the dunes now acts as a focal point for the whole of this extremely suitable site for terns, which have nested there since 1839. The warden usually lives at the Point during summer months, and has several helpers in order to show people where they can, or cannot, go during the busy nesting period.

'Holkham Bay'
A great bay that attracts so many thousands of people during the year to enjoy walking among the dunes and the marram grass.

Being the most northerly point on the Norfolk coast, and practically an island, this Point is an excellent place to observe many of the great migratory flocks coming into England in autumn. Several rare species are seen regularly by the birdwatchers here, and the harbour, being surrounded by saltmarshes, is the haunt of many types of duck. Among them the lovely distinctive wigeon, with its whistling calls, and, of course, big flocks of brent geese.

and rarer little terns have a yellow bill and legs; and the larger sandwich terns, which are very striking, have a large black crest, a black bill tipped with yellow, and also black legs. These birds have always been referred to as sea swallows, and when hovering over the water for small fish or sand eels, they will suddenly drop with a plop, and in a flash rise again with their catch. They have remarkably good eyesight. Their eggs are laid in scrapes in the sand or shingle, and the nests, difficult to observe as they are, mean that the young chicks or eggs can be trodden on. Heavy rain or high seas can also flood the nests. In some seasons the total number of chicks raised can be very

'Holkham Bay'

On the shingle banks and dunes are the terns, the gulls and the waders. On a fine spring morning, or early summer, you are in sight of the white flashing wings of the terns overhead. They keep up a continuous movement at their nesting sites. There are two hides from which the birds can be watched, so that they are not disturbed.

The delightful common terns have red legs and an orange bill with a black tip; the much smaller

low. Their nesting sites are out of bounds to visitors, and should anyone approach too close to their nests, the parent birds will divebomb, and they can even strike an intruder.

In the far north of Norway, when I lived there with the Lapps, we were on a small island one day, and the arctic terns would divebomb our little group in the same way. The Lapps collected the eggs and boiled them in an old kettle over a wood fire

'Looking towards Blakeney Point is a favourite spot at Morston, from which boats make the trip daily to see the seals and stop at the Point.'

HUGH BRANDON-FOX

among the vegetation. There were no nature reserves in that mass of small uninhabited islands.

The National Trust has produced an excellent colour booklet called *Blakeney Point*, giving a good description of everything to be found there. The large number of different plants are shown and good colour photographs of the birds. You should certainly acquire one of the booklets when you go to the Point.

Quite close in the waters around the Point, and a source of great attraction to all visitors, is a permanent colony of common and grey seals. Numbering up to about 400 or so, they breed in the spits there, with the common pups being born between June and August. The grey seal pups are born between October and December. The ferry-boats go as close as possible for a good view. Seals have always had an appeal wherever they are found round our coasts, and despite natural reductions in some years, their numbers are fairly consistent.

The little port of Blakeney itself has a tremendously long history. There are so many fascinating facts about this coastal village, which is now very popular, especially in the summer months. Around this area, the silting up of the channels has always been a problem, and it was the 17th century that really saw the beginning of the end of trading at Cley and Wiveton, which were quite prosperous ports in those days. This had near disastrous results for Blakeney as well.

Salthouse and Cley marshes had been drained in 1522 and this had altered the flow in Cley channel. In 1630 a Dutchman began enclosing the marshes at Salthouse, while seven years later there was a similar exercise on the Blakeney marshes.

There is a raised embankment, which was actually built in 1650, along which you can walk today to see the saltmarshes, and way out to the mud-flats. But the boats, when they became larger, were unable to reach Blakeney quay. The coastal trade, however, was still strong, and in 1786 the combined port of Blakeney and Cley was given the status of chief port. Smuggling was very strong at that time, and this was possibly a means of trying to control it.

At the beginning of this century Blakeney was a tough and rough place really to live, and about a

'Blakeney Evening'

'Good sailing days make life along the coast a great attraction for thousands of enthusiasts.'

quarter of the population were employed in or around the quay. At that time it was filled with boats busily loading and unloading corn, coal, fertilisers, cattle food, malt and other goods which were trundled up the narrow streets of the, then, very active village. Today, of course, all this is gone, and the bustle comes from the many visitors who delight in the narrow streets and the sense of the past still resonant in Blakeney.

The ferry-boats taking visitors over to Blakeney Point, as they do from Morston, leave the quayside when the tide is full enough. It is a short journey, but one full of interest, and when you arrive at the Point and disembark there, you can gaze at a wonderful vista all the way along the coastline. Small boats of every description fill the channel these days and this whole area is a real change for people who come from large towns or cities and appreciate everything, from the tang of the salt air, to the wide open views to the far horizon.

There is one body for whom I have the greatest admiration and respect for their work in preserving the wildlife of Norfolk. It is the Norfolk Wildlife Trust, established in 1926 by Dr Sydney Long, who was able to purchase 407 acres of the Cley marshes to set up a trust 'as a bird breeding sanctuary for all time', when it was then the first ever county conservation trust. There are now, of course, a great many more coming under the aegis of the Royal Society for Nature Conservation.

Cley marshes, which were the first reserve to be bought by the Trust, are now the real mecca for birdwatchers at any time of the year. The work of managing all the various reserves that this Trust now owns is worthy of the greatest praise, and under the supervision of their present director, Brendan Joyce, the Trust goes from strength to strength in its determination to preserve the wildlife in this county, which is so valuable to the whole of national nature conservation.

Cley itself, on the east side of the river Glaven, is now separated from the sea by marshlands, but was a flourishing fishing and trading port in earlier days. The marshes were steadily being reclaimed during the 17th and 18th centuries, but the creeks and the river had already begun to silt up. The Customs and Excise office closed in 1853, and the smuggling, which had been so strong at Blakeney and Cley, gradually disappeared.

The distinctive windmill at Cley, which was built in 1819, is now open to the public, and also offers the chance of staying there for holidays. It makes a really excellent point from which to explore the area. After a walk on Cley marshes, which can be quite tiring, I have found a charming place to either drink or eat – or both. It is The Three Swallows public house at Newgate Green.

The coastal region has a great number of very historic and beautiful small churches which are still well attended.

HUGH BRANDON-COX

For many years now there has been discussion about making a better sea wall along the Cley marshes. A big shingle bank has kept out most of the storms, but at times the floods have come over and brought deep flooding over the grazing marshes and even on to the road and into some of the houses at Salthouse. Now it is proposed that a big sea wall be made inside that shingle bank going all the way right through to Cley marshes. In the course of a few years the whole scheme will have become history but for the moment it will mean upheaval and disruption of a lot of the marsh area and the birds that visit there. The existing shingle bank will still remain but it will be allowed to change to a broader lower profile and is expected to roll inland in time. What it will all mean is that the flooding

'Midwinter - Fishing in the Cley Reeds'

'Nothing is more attractive to the eye than geese coming back to the saltings in the glow of dusk.'

Hugh BRANDON-Cox

will hopefully stop and the scheme is considered well worth all the effort and trouble – particularly by the residents of Salthouse.

The tremendous amount of clay that will be needed to build this wall will be obtained from shallow pits dug in the grazing marshes. The scheme will really result in a big change to the appearance of the nature reserve at Cley and Salthouse and instead of the wide sweeping view that we now have we shall be staring at quite a high wall in the course of time. As it was stated in *Tern* magazine, there has been a tremendous amount of co-operative work put in to ensure that this bank will be thought out and very carefully undertaken so that it will disrupt as little as possible the whole work of the much valued reserve. The work will have to be undertaken during the fine months of spring and summer when the diggers can work at their best. Neither the brent geese, that I have painted so many times and love to see so much, nor the wigeon with their great beauty, will be there at that time so there will be no disruption to their visit. It will, I am sure, all be for the best. If we look back through the years there has been, since the time of the first reserves, change and possible disruption at first, but everything has turned out for the benefit of the wildlife which is being so carefully preserved by all these bodies.

This extremely important reserve is efficiently managed by Bernard Bishop, who lives in what is called the Watcher's Cottage, from where you can obtain permits to visit the various hides. The Bishop family has a long history of looking after and managing this big area. First of all it was Robert Bishop, who from 1926 until 1937 was a sort of keeper-manager. Then came Billy Bishop, who eventually retired in 1979, and the task has now been taken over by his son Bernard in turn, and a mighty fine job he does too. Not only are there the marshes and grazing land to look after but a huge reed-bed to be cut and managed as well.

One of the great attractions of this reserve now is the large colony of striking black and white avocets successfully returning to England after a long absence. Now they regularly rear each year a large batch of young. Years ago when I was a boy, there was no restriction on people going and collecting birds' eggs, of course. I grew up on the saltings around St Osyth in Essex where I had a small boat. There we had a large colony of black-headed gulls, and I collected their eggs in a small bucket to bring home to my grandmother, who made good use of them in cakes and puddings! They had a bright orange yolk and a very strong taste. Of course, the gulls tired of this eventually, and moved the whole flock somewhere away to a quieter position. I only mention this because of the great necessity today to see that eggs are not stolen from any of these birds, especially those of the avocets that are so welcome here. The warden endeavours so much to preserve the area in which they can breed on the Cley marshes.

'The elegant and graceful avocets are now nesting at several of the reserves. They are warmly welcomed back each spring after a long absence from the Norfolk coast.'

'Land of the Mussel Growers'

Michael Seago, who wrote very informative articles on birds of Britain in the *Eastern Daily Press*, quotes something that I think is interesting and will bear out what I have just said. He writes, 'It is fascinating to find references in Victorian volumes that one of the Salthouse gunners regularly filled his cap, coat pockets, and even his stockings with avocet eggs for puddings and pancakes.' A similar hostile reception overcame the remaining Suffolk colony at Orfordness.

The birds disappeared from England for a long time after that, and it was enormously pleasurable to find them coming back to our Norfolk coastal reserves such as Cley and Titchwell. Their nests are on sandy or muddy banks, and are, of course, always in danger of flooding. If that happens the pairs will build quite substantial structures. When the nestlings are born, they are able to leave the nest after a few hours of hatching. Bernard Bishop tells

me that in 1992 there were 44 pairs nesting, and 85 young were reared, which was very good, but in 1993 we had a particularly unpleasant and wet time during the breeding season, and this depleted the numbers being hatched and fledged. Residents of the Norfolk coast are always at the mercy of the weather.

Norfolk reed has always been renowned for its lasting quality and strength. The Wildlife Trust has about 1000 acres of reed-beds in the county, all of which have to be managed for the high quality reeds they produce, and for the welfare of the wildlife. There is a team busy all through January and February at Cley, cutting the reed for which there is a great demand. Norfolk still produces about half of Britain's reeds, but it amazes me that this country which used to be so self-sufficient in reeds, now imports a great amount of its needs. As farmers are encouraged these days to produce fewer food crops,

'The handsome and colourful shelducks can be seen along the reed-beds at Cley. They nest in burrows among the dunes.'

HUGH BRANDON-6x

could reed growing be a sound alternative to leaving the land fallow? It is a slow process, however, and the growers themselves need to do more research to make it commercially viable.

Reed-beds at Cley have to be cut before it is time for such birds as the reed and sedge warblers, reed buntings and even the lovely little bearded tits to nest there. A substantial number of birds can be supported in the reeds because of the large population of insects. In the winter the reed's seed, which is produced in large quantities, provides food for the bearded tits. Recently cut reed-beds are often used by snipe, and they now hold significant numbers of these birds, who have often disappeared from other grazing marshes.

One of the rarest sights, of course, is the bittern, which is a reed-bed specialist. Having a wonderful camouflage and a booming call which echoes for long distances, it was once eaten as a delicacy at Christmas. Those days are gone, and somehow it just manages to survive in some of the Norfolk reed-beds.

Without cutting, many of the beds outside nature reserves would be dominated by willow and alder, and the birds that they support would, of course, have disappeared. It is hard work cutting and preparing reeds for dispatch to the many places where there is a good demand, but it is worth it to the Wildlife Trust, helping to meet some of their huge costs.

Moving directly on from Cley we come to the big Salthouse marshes. This is the last of the reserves along this coastal route. Here the management of the marshes themselves mostly relies on the farmers. Their sheep, horses, and cattle graze throughout the summer, maintaining the open plant communities. This prevents the fields from becoming an accumulation of dead vegetation. If you are fortunate, you may have a sight of the barn owls that frequently quarter these fields, and possibly the hen harriers, which are a lovely sight at any time. This reserve is similar to the others in its various aspects, and with good fortune, you can see a wide variety of birds and plants.

Mankind has been the great destroyer of so much of the natural beauty of this world. The balance of nature is very fragile. Left alone, nature, we have always felt, would balance itself. But now, with the enormous and increasing demand for more and more roads, and ever larger airports, we must be thankful indeed that this coastal strip of Norfolk is at least preserved and in good hands.

The journey along this coast will give you great pleasure at all times of the year, and provide all the adventure that you need without travelling from these shores. I leave you to wander, as I have so many times, over the saltings, the mud-flats and the sands of north Norfolk, whether it be bright sunshine or a howling wind. The memories will remain for a very long time.

Hugh Brandon-Cox

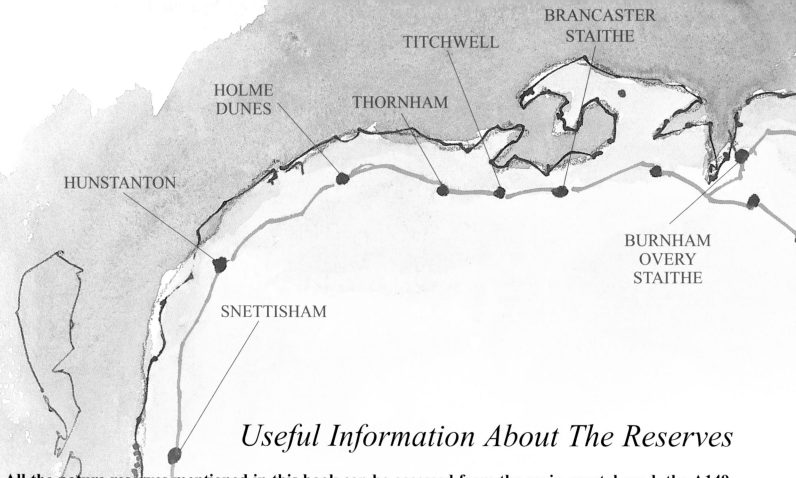

BRANCASTER
STAITHE

TITCHWELL

HOLME
DUNES

THORNHAM

HUNSTANTON

BURNHAM
OVERY
STAITHE

SNETTISHAM

Useful Information About The Reserves

All the nature reserves mentioned in this book can be accessed from the main coastal road, the A149, and are fully signposted.

RSPB, Snettisham

There is a large car park and public toilets which are usually open. To the left there is approximately a mile of stiff walking before one gets to the hides. Visitors with disabilities are welcome at Snettisham but please call to discuss access arrangements, Tel. 01485 542689. Car parking is £2.00.

Hunstanton

Please ring the Tourist Information Centre on 01485 532610, for all information about birds and various places to visit there.

Holme Dunes

There are public toilets and a very long walk along the dunes near the golf course. For members of the Norfolk Wildlife Trust there is a road leading to the central office and various hides overlooking the lakes where one can even see the avocets nesting in the summer.

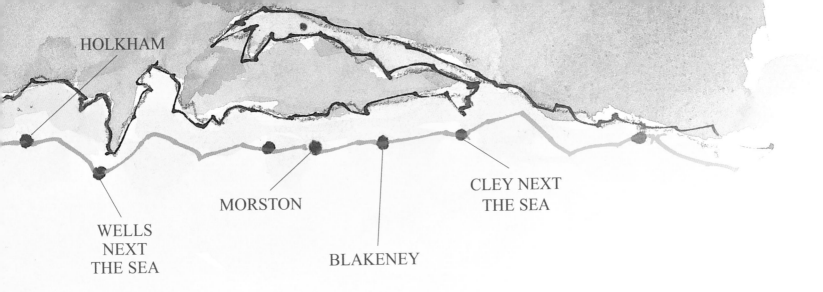

Thornham
One can park along the quay side but there are no other facilities at this reserve.

Titchwell
Titchwell has its own bus stop. Call Travel Line on 0870 6082608 for all public transport enquiries. There are free cycle racks outside the Titchwell Visitor Centre, car parking here costs £3.00 but is free for RSPB members. There are toilets for the Nature Reserve visitors in the car park at Titchwell. Light snacks are also available. For further information telephone 01485 210779.

Brancaster Staithe
The main attraction here is the natural harbour created by the saltmarshes and Scolt Head Island, which is owned by the National Trust, and a very good outlet for sailing. Courses are available for schools at the National Trust Brancaster Activity Centre, tel. 01485 210719 for full details and a brochure. There are public toilets near the activity centre for walkers.

Burnham Overy Staithe
One can take a boat here to Scolt Head. There are regular visits all according to the time of the tide. There are no public toilets here. A very long raised footpath gives fine views all the way along this magnificent creek.

Holkham

Access to the very large magnificent Holkham Bay and two hides is from Lady Anne's Drive. There is a £2.00 charge. There are no toilet facilities at all on this reserve. The nearest would be at Wells. For full information about this and Holkham Hall, tel. 01328 710227.

Wells Next The Sea

For all general information about this extremely interesting port, tel. 01328 710885.

Morston

An immensely popular place this. One takes the various boats here either to Blakeney Point or to see the seals. The times may vary according to the state of the tide and weather but it is very rare that the boats are not well filled, so be aware of the car park being rather full. The very many trips daily are run by three families. Bishop's Boats go from Morston and Blakeney, tel. 01263 740753. Both Graham and John Bean Boats go over to the Point and on the seal trips, their telephone number is 01263 740505 and 740038. Then there is the Temple Ferry Service which is also from Morston Quay and that is 01263 740791. During the summer months light refreshments and ice creams can be bought from a travelling van on the quayside and there is also a very good pub, The Anchor, which can serve you really excellent meals. There are also toilets there.

Blakeney

A large car park from which there is a raised path that goes all the way down the creek and branches off, making an almost circular walk to Cley Mill of about two miles. Delightful place to shop here with 'old world' buildings, but be aware in the middle of summer, it is very, very crowded.

Cley Next The Sea

The real Mecca for the birdwatchers. There is an excellent raised visitor centre from which one has a wonderful view over the whole of the reserve, the reeds and also the hides, which have been made with thatch and fit in perfectly with the surroundings. This reserve is the oldest in the country and has just celebrated its 75th year and it started a national movement of now 47 wildlife trusts and over 2000 nature reserves. The marshes are open every day except Christmas day and Boxing day. The visitor centre is open from April to early December, telephone 01263 740008. Wheelchair access to many of the bird hides and group bookings are welcome. There are toilet facilities at the visitor centre from which it is also possible to obtain coffee and ice cream.